Albany James Christie

Union with Rome

Five afternoon lectures

Albany James Christie

Union with Rome
Five afternoon lectures

ISBN/EAN: 9783741183744

Manufactured in Europe, USA, Canada, Australia, Japa

Cover: Foto ©Thomas Meinert / pixelio.de

Manufactured and distributed by brebook publishing software
(www.brebook.com)

Albany James Christie

Union with Rome

UNION WITH ROME.

Five Afternoon Lectures

PREACHED IN

The Church of the Immaculate Conception, Farm Street.

BY THE

REV. ALBANY J. CHRISTIE.

Of the Society of Jesus.

PUBLISHED BY REQUEST.

LONDON:
BURNS, OATES, AND COMPANY, 17, PORTMAN STREET,
AND PATERNOSTER ROW.

1869.

CONTENTS.

LECTURE I.

THE CASE STATED.

THERE is one point on which all who call themselves Christians are agreed—namely, that the actual state of Christendom is a state of disunion, and to be lamented. The fact of this disunion is admitted by all, for it is too obvious to be denied, but there is a difference of opinion with respect to the nature and effects of this disunion. It is the doctrine of Christians in union with the Holy See, that this disunion involves the separation of certain bodies of men from the vital centre, so that while that centre, with all that are united to it, is the true living Body of Christ, those communities which have separated from it have ceased to be, as communities, living portions of Christ's Body; while the central stock, with the various branches united with it, is the Vine of Christ, those other branches, once (but now no longer) united with the stock, are cut-off branches, dead and dried up, and incapable, as branches, of communicating grace to those individuals who belong to them. In the opinion of Anglicans, this disunion of Christendom consists in the standing aloof of various Churches of Christendom from each other, while, notwithstanding, they still continue to be living branches—living Churches —because, by the nature (as they deem) of the Church,

B

each Bishop is of right independent of the rest, and each diocese under its proper Bishop has all that is essential to constitute it a Church, even though it may be separated from all other Churches.

From these two positions two different views are taken of the manner in which the restoration to unity is to be brought about. According to one view, any person who is a member of a separated body is bound to leave the body in which he finds himself, and to attach himself to that one only body which is the true Church of Christ. In the Anglican view, since, it is said, each local Church is independent and a true Church—though from unhappy circumstances separated from its sister Churches—it is not necessary for its individual members to leave it, as though there were only one Church into whose bosom they should return, but its individual members should promote as far as they are able the desirable object of reunion, while they should themselves wait until the body to which they belong can make terms and unite with its equally independent sisters.

Hence the Anglican theory of corporate reunion ; a theory founded on an utter misapprehension of the nature of the unity of the Church of God—the last resource of men who, with a well meant but mistaken loyalty, cling to that which is miscalled the Church of their Baptism, and which debars so very many souls from finding peace and truth in the true fold of Christ. It is my wish to-day to state sincerely the Anglican theory, and to contrast it with the Catholic, and to exhibit the truth of the Catholic theory in general, while we may enter into a more detailed exhibition of its truth in the subsequent lectures. The relation of sisters to each other without a father to guide them will represent the Anglican view; the union of sisters under a father, the Catholic view.

Anglicans, no less than Catholics, teach that there is a visible Church; but Anglicans teach that the several parts which make up this Church are *independent*. Catholics teach that the several parts which make up this Church are *dependent* upon *one visible Head*. The words which characterise and may distinguish the two theories, are "independence" and "dependence." Anglicans insist on independence; Catholics teach dependence. Surely, at the very outset, the Christian ought to discern here the spirit of evil and the spirit of good. Who are they who make much of independence? Is it the spirit of Christ or the spirit of the world? Who are they who love to be dependent? Is it not they who are led by the spirit of Christ? Of course the world, and Catholics too who have been contaminated by the spirit of the world, will find something attractive in the word independence; of course human nature, unaided by grace, will rise in rebellion against the notion of dependence. But, let the truth be told, independence and dependence characterise the two opposing theories, and when we recollect that our Master, the only Being entitled to independence, was so enamoured of humility and dependence as to become dependent on His own creatures—when we recollect His teaching, that we must become as little children to enter into the Kingdom of God—we shall not be ashamed of the Gospel of Christ, which is the power of God unto

B 2

salvation, and we shall find in our dependence the true liberty of the children of God.

Anglicans teach that the several parts of which the visible Church is composed are *independent.* Each several part consists of its own Bishop with his Clergy and the flock committed to him ; and every Bishop with his Clergy and flock constitute a Church, possessed of all that is necessary, so far as external government is concerned, for its integrity. Hence, however desirable it may be that unity should exist among the different Bishops and their Churches—however lamentable the separation of one from another—yet, if circumstances have brought about this severance from each other, this does not affect the several parts in such a way as to interfere with their true character as Churches of Christ. It follows therefore that while the Bishop of Rome with his Roman diocese forms a true Church, so does the Bishop of Paris with his diocese, and the Bishop of Armagh with his ; each one is independent of the other, no one has any special right over another, and it is no more necessary for the integrity of the Church of Armagh that the Bishop of Armagh should be in communion with Rome, than it is for the integrity of the Church and diocese of Rome that it should be in communion with Armagh. It is desirable that they should be in union ; but, they say, it is not necessary nor essential to their character as Churches.

Hence, according to the Anglican theory, the unity of the Church would consist in a confederation of inde-pendent Churches. It is a theory which applies to Bishops the principle which Anglicans themselves con-demn when applied to individual laymen by those who

are called Independents among Dissenters—a theory
contrary to the promises of Christ, contrary to the very
intention of the Church ; a theory proved by facts to
be the source of confusion, and destructive of the fulfilment of the Church's office. This will be shown on
future Sundays.

Catholics teach that the several parts of which the
Church is composed are not independent, but dependent
—dependent on a visible centre, on a visible Head.
Each Bishop has his own diocese, his own flock ; but
among all Bishops, one has been chosen to be the
visible representative of Christ, the Chief Bishop ;
among all Churches, one has been chosen to be that
centre, by union with which the unity of the whole
Church is to be secured. Who that Bishop should be,
it rested with Jesus Christ to determine. He might
have selected James, or John, or Andrew, but in fact
He chose Peter, and while He associated him with
them in all the privileges he conferred on them, He
singled him out and gave him privileges which He did
not grant to them. He made him a *foundation* of His
Church, as He did each of them ; but besides He made
Peter, by name and office, *Rock*, associating him with
Himself in this special privilege. What city that should
be which should give its name to the see by union with
which all other Churches are to be formed into one
Church, depended on God's providence, which should
determine what see St. Peter should hold, and where
he should die. It might have been Jerusalem, or
Ephesus, or Antioch, or Naples, but in fact it was
Rome, and it will be Rome till the time when the
Church militant shall cease to be, and be merged into

the Church triumphant. Such is the teaching of Catholics, and it is plain that according to this teaching the Church of Christ is not a confederation of independent Churches, but one Church, comparable to a body in which there is a head and many members, all the members being subordinate to that head—the Invisible Head, Christ, the visible, His Vicegerent; comparable to a vine, in which there is a trunk or stock, and attached to it many branches, which would lose all their fecundity if they were cut off; comparable, not to a federation like that of America, but to a kingdom. And is it not called the *Kingdom of Heaven?* which implies the existence of one at the head of the rest, and a government which, though it admits of assemblies of Bishops in Councils of various kinds, implies also the paternal government of one who is invested with authority over all the rest. Surely the very statement of the Catholic teaching brings home to our minds its agreement with the principles contained in Holy Scripture in all that it says with relation to the constitution of the Church. The body, the vine, the kingdom, all point to a unity which is not represented by the federation of independent Churches pleaded for by Anglicans, but to the compactness which can be secured only by the existence of some visible centre of unity, such as is taught by Catholics.

Such then are the two theories of the constitution of the Church, and of its unity. Such is the *primâ facie* recommendation of the Catholic representation over the Anglican. But now, before entering more in detail into the untenableness of the Anglican system, there is something which ought certainly to be pre-

mised. It is this: even though the Anglican system
of independent Churches were true, it would not secure
the Anglican, or justify his continuance in Anglicanism.
And why?

Because the Anglican Bishops are no true Bishops,
and, therefore, if for no other reason, the Anglican
Churches can be no true Churches. Take the very
lowest consideration. There is at least doubt about
Anglican Orders. No corporate reunion then *can* take
place, for it would be impossible for the Church of
Rome, whose Orders are certain, to admit the Orders
of Anglicans while the doubt remains. It is sufficiently
terrible for us to know that there are thousands of
Ministers pretending to consecrate bread and wine in
their Communion service; it would be still worse were
we to give our sanction to their proceedings. Were the
doctrine of independent Churches admissible, it would
apply to the Greek schismatics, but not to the Anglicans; for the Orders of the Greeks are valid, while
those of the Anglicans are at the least doubtful, and, as
we believe, invalid.

Another consequence is this—that every Anglican
is bound to embrace the communion of the Catholic
Church, were it only that the Orders of the Catholic
Church are certain, while he must have some mis-
giving about Anglican Orders. He *is* sure that our
Bishops are real Bishops, our Priests real Priests, and
that our Sacraments are all valid Sacraments. He has
no question about the matter, and he knows that no
one else has any question about the matter. On the
other hand, he knows that, however desirous he is to
believe the Anglican Bishops to be Bishops and the

Anglican Priests to be Priests, yet, whatever *he* thinks, the great body of Christians throughout the world deny the Anglican Orders, and *they* may, after all, be right and *he* wrong; and therefore, in a matter of so much moment as Sacraments, an Anglican is bound to join that Church where he is sure that the Communion of our Lord's Body and Blood is not doubtful, and abandon that religious body in which, at least, it is doubtful.

Here, before concluding to-day, I would secure myself against a misapprehension. I say that the theory of independent Bishops and independent Churches is un-Christian, un-Scriptural, and false ; that the Church of Christ is not a federation of independent Churches, but that all true Churches are made one Church by union with and dependence on the visible centre instituted by Christ Himself, and that all who are not in union with that centre are bound to unite themselves to it without waiting for a corporate reunion which is impossible. Is it, then, to be said that all who are external to the visible unity of the Church are lost ; and that none but those who return into the bosom of the fold of which St. Peter, in his successor, is the Chief Pastor after Christ, the chief visible Pastor—will see God in peace ? The answer is plain. For those who have every means afforded them of knowing and entering the one visible fold, it is absolutely necessary that they should enter it. But, if you ask me whether any will come to salvation without external union with the one visible Church of Christ, I answer that I am sure there may be many, and the reason for this belief is contained in at once God's justice and God's mercy.

Through His mercy Christ died for all and merited grace for all. He purchased with His own Blood His visible Church, and made that Church infallible in truth and the dispenser of grace in the holy sacraments, and blessed are they who are her faithful children. But it is a fact that thousands—nay, millions—have no means of acquaintance with this Church, or else are brought up with the idea that this Church is superstitious and idolatrous. What is to become of these? Why these, too, receive graces through the merits of the Cross of Christ, and, for certain, if they make use of these graces, they will share in the glory which is their natural termination. But with us the question is not whether pagans in India, or Protestants who have never entered a Catholic church, can be saved without union with the visible Head of the Church, but a question far more practical. It is whether *we*, dear brethren in Christ, could be saved were we to renounce that unity, and whether those of you who hear me now and are not in this unity could be saved without embracing it. Others may be outside the visible Church, unconnected with her visible Head, without any fault of their own, but could this be said of *you?* If there are some here now who have been reared with distorted notions of the Catholic Church, the very fact of your finding yourselves, now perhaps for the first time, in a Catholic church ; hearing, perhaps for the first time, the case stated between Anglicanism and Catholicity—this fact, is enough to lead you to reflection, and if you reflect, you, who have been hitherto unconsciously in error, will find the truth approve itself to you, and you will find yourselves drawn to enter the one visible fold of the

True Shepherd, and enter into communion with its visible Head; to enter the Kingdom of God on earth, which, as a visible kingdom, has a visible Head; to be reunited to the Body of Christ, of which, as the limbs are visible, so is the Head, and which cannot suffer division without the death of the limb that is separated from it.

Next Sunday I hope to state clearly and briefly the proof that the Church of Christ on earth is one, not by the federation of a number of independent Churches, but by the union of all Churches under one visible Head. The end for which the Church was founded requires such a unity, the promises of Christ require it, and the events which are taking place around us among those who are called by the name of Christians prove that the other system is ruinous and fatal.

LECTURE II.

Come to Me all ye that labour and are burdened and I will refresh you.—
St. Matt. xi. 28.

How, in few words, might we describe the Christian faith? God looked down from Heaven on the children of men; He saw them all wandering out of the way, and He resolved to work their salvation. He came down from Heaven and became as one of them. While on earth He with His own lips taught the truth; He forgave sins and gave grace. As man He must die; and He died on the Cross to atone for sin, and to make us hate the sin for which he suffered; and He ascended to Heaven, but He did not leave His work imperfect. That which He did in His own Person while on earth He continued, through the Church, after His ascension. He taught through her the truth; through her He forgave sins; and through her, in the sacraments, He gave grace. Because it was *men* that He taught and forgave and blessed, He existed *visibly* as man; and because it is *men* who have to be taught and forgiven and blessed to the end of the world, His Church is *visible*; and because the truth which she teaches is *one*, and, notwithstanding, liable to be distorted in a thousand ways, the visible Church is *one* also.

It is agreed by Catholics and Anglicans that the Church of Christ is a visible society ; it is agreed by both that this visible society is territorially divided into parts, and that each of these parts has its own divinely-appointed visible Pastor, who is called the Bishop. Then comes the point of difference. Catholics teach that all these Bishops are united into one body by their dependence on a divinely-appointed Chief Pastor, who is the visible representative of the Church's ascended visible Head ; Anglicans deny this, and deny the existence of any such divinely-appointed visible Head, and claim independence for each local Bishop.

Here a serious and fundamental error of Anglicans has to be noticed. They admit that, by ecclesiastical law, Bishops may be arranged under Metropolitans, and Metropolitans under Patriarchs, and that, were all the Patriarchs assembled, a complimentary priority might be granted to the Pope, but they affirm that all this is matter of ecclesiastical law, and not of divine right. Hence, as in disunion between a Bishop and his Metropolitan, divine right is not infringed, and however much the disunion may be lamented, the suffragan Church loses nothing of the essentials of a Church, but retains them no less than its Metropolitan. As the same may be said of the relation of a Bishop to his Patriarch— disunion would be lamentable, but the separated Bishop, with his diocese, would continue a living branch—so ought the same, according to Anglicans, to be said of the relation of a Bishop with the Pope. Separation is to be regretted, reunion to be desired, but still, notwithstanding the division, say, between the Church of Rome and the Church of Corsica, the Church of Rome would remain a true Church and the Church of Corsica would remain a true Church, and it would be wrong for persons in the Church of Corsica to seek, as individuals, reunion with Rome — they ought to wait for the corporate reunion of the two Churches.

Here there is a fatal error, a confusion of two matters utterly distinct, namely, of ecclesiastical human law and of divine law. There is, indeed, no institution of Metropolitans or Patriarchs in the fundamental constitution of the Church of Christ, but there is divine institution of Bishops and divine institution of one Chief Pastor, their visible Head and bond of union. These two elements—the Episcopate and the visible Headship —are necessary ; Metropolitans and Patriarchs are convenient. These two elements are necessary to secure those two notes of the Church called its Catholicity and its Unity. Because the Church is Catholic, and exists in every clime under heaven, there is need of the Episcopate, of Bishops to feed the flock that has to be shared among them ; because it is One, all those flocks with their Pastors need a centre of union, a visible Headship to which they must be attached. Between these two extremes—the Bishops and the chief visible Pastor, convenience and ecclesiastical law may institute intermediate grades, differing not in kind but in degree from the episcopal, but the very essence of the Church of Christ requires the multiplicity of the Episcopate and the unity of the Headship. And yet it cannot but be feared that many have been deceived by the seeming argument derived from the successive subordination of dignity among Bishops. They admit the divine institution of Bishops, and they see that Bishops are

·clustered under Metropolitans, and that Metropolitans exist only for convenience of government; then they see Metropolitans clustered under Patriarchs, and still no one requires them to regard the institution of Patriarchs as of other than ecclesiastical law; and then they fall into the error of passing the same judgment on the visible Head of the Church himself, ignorant that his office is ·as essential to the visible Church as the Episcopate is, and that it utterly differs from that of Metropolitans and Patriarchs in its necessity, which is absolute, and its institution, which is divine. I would remark that this distinction renders nugatory a principal argument in the work of a well-known Anglican author, who labours hard to prove that the English Church is no part of the Roman Patriarchate. Be it so; suppose it were not; what matters it? **No** Catholic asserts the necessity of the union of **the** English Church with the successors of St. Peter on the ground ·that the Roman Church is the Patriarchal Church of England, but because St. Peter and his successors are, by the divine institution of Jesus Christ, the visible Head of the Kingdom of Heaven, or the Church, on earth, and so of all Bishops under whatever Patriarchs, and of the Patriarchs themselves.

The following propositions shall now be made good: (1.) It is *à priori* probable that the visible Church of Christ should have a visible Head; (2.) a visible Head was expressly given to it by Jesus Christ; and (3.) the facts we see around us confirm the necessity of its existence.

1. When the antecedent probability of a visible Head to the Church of Christ is asserted, it is meant that

on the grounds which are admitted alike by Catholics and Protestants, the necessity of a visible Head is reasonably inferred.

Our Blessed Lord set on foot a society called in the Creed the One, Holy, Catholic and Apostolic Church; the figure of a net, a body, a sheepfold, a vine, a kingdom, all point to the unity of this society, and the prayer of our Blessed Lord for His Church just before His Passion is emphatic on this characteristic of unity. "I pray," He said to the Eternal Father, "that they may be one as we also are one" (St. John xvii.). How would ordinary human prudence provide for the right management of a society organised for carrying out a certain definite end, and intended to be characterised by unity. Independent nations, indeed, may be associated for particular objects, but such a union does not produce unity; if States are joined together in a confederation, the only chance of their non-dissolution is the existence of a central bond, such as a president. Charitable associations, like that of St. Vincent of Paul, form one association because they acknowledge one President, with his Central Council. Religious Orders, if they are severally to be *one*, must look up to and acknowledge one General Superior. And if we look to the enemies of God, we shall find that they are wise in their generation, and that the secret societies form one compact anti-Christian army by their recognition of a central head. If, then, Jesus Christ would institute a visible society whereof one note was to be unity, it would not have been in accordance with His wisdom to leave that society without a visible Head. Besides, the office of the

Church as the Teacher of *truth* after the ascension of
our Lord requires a real unity with a recognised centre.
Truth is one, and there needs a centre to which all the
teachings of the various local Churches may converge,
in order to exclude the spoiling of truth. Now, it is
certain that no Bishops, by virtue of their Episcopal
character,. have been secured from error ; the Bishop
of Rome, as such, is no more secure than any other
·Bishop by virtue of his Episcopal character. He
had been already consecrated *Bishop*, before he was
elected to be the successor of St. Peter; it is then
probable that another privilege should be granted which
should protect truth, and that some visible Head should
be selected, which by the assistance of the Holy Ghost
should be preserved from error.

2. If then, *à priori*, it is accordant with the wisdom
of the Founder of a universal visible Church to provide
a visible Head for the preservation of unity and truth,
it would be inaccordant with wisdom on our part to
explain away testimonies of Holy Scripture which
certainly, in their simple obvious sense, fall in with
such antecedent probability ; we should not set any
value on those subterfuges by which men, who whether
consciously or unconsciously are swayed by the necessity of defending their own position, strive to elude the
force of proofs which simple honesty will confess to be
conclusive. We shall not be persuaded that it was
for nothing that the very first moment that our Lord
set eyes on Simon, He said, "Thou shalt be called
Cephas"—*i.c.*, Rock. We shall not be persuaded to
believe that when our Lord was on the point of
announcing His departure (St. Matt. xvi. 21), and of

providing for His absence, He said with no special
meaning to Simon, " Thou art Cephas (rock), and on
this Cephas (rock), I will build My Church ; " or that,
when He said, " *On this Cephas* I will build My
Church," He pointed with His Hand to Himself; a
mode of explaining Scripture by which any meaning
may be educed out of anything. We shall not be
persuaded that when He said to Simon again, " I will
give to thee the keys of the Kingdom of Heaven,"
that He did not mean, " I will give to thee authority
over My Church." We shall not be persuaded, when
He was just on the point of ascending to Heaven,
and of withdrawing His own visible presence, that He
meant nothing by the thrice-repeated charge He gave
to Peter separately from the rest of the Apostles
(St. John xxi. 15, &c.).

Indeed, so strong are the expressions of our Blessed
Lord, that it is true to assert that divine as is the
authority of the Priesthood, divine as is the authority
of the Episcopate, the Scriptural proof, contained in
the words of Jesus Christ Himself, of the authority
given to St. Peter as ruler of Christ's Church, as
Christ's visible Vicar, is far stronger than that of either
the Episcopal or the Sacerdotal ; and in order to meet
a difficulty which might arise in the mind of an
Anglican—namely, that though the supremacy were
granted to St. Peter, it does not follow that it survived
him—it is to be remarked that the *nature* of the proof
of the visible Headship of the Church is the same as
that for the Episcopate. The proof of both, prescinding
from the Church's authority, rests on this, that such
as was the constitution of the Church in the essentials

c

of its government in the Apostles' time, such it was to
continue to the end.   But, argue the Episcopalians,
in the Apostles' time there was the Episcopal office
and government, therefore the Episcopal government
which we find in later times is only the necessary
continuation of the primitive Church government ; so
Catholics see the continuance of the divine institution
not only in the Episcopate, but in the visible Headship
of the Episcopate granted to St. Peter and continued
to his successors.   The Catholicity of the Church
required the Episcopate, its Unity required the visible
Headship.   The reason for the one was as cogent as
the reason for the other, and as the Church spread and
heretics· arose, the reason for the visible Headship grew
more cogent still.

3. The antecedent probability of the appointment
of a visible Head, and the proof derived from our
Blessed Lord's own words to St. Peter, receive con-
firmation from the *facts* that in the present day surround
us.   They clearly show that the Catholic teaching, and
not the Anglican view, agrees with the above-named
conditions necessary for the Church founded by Christ.
The conditions are unity and truth, and actual facts
will lay bare the evasions resorted to in the attempts
to exhibit Anglicanism as a true branch of Christ's
Church ; facts will prove that unity on the Anglican
theory is only another name for disunion, and that
truth on the same theory is self-contradictory.   As to
unity, the Creed calls the Church One.   Is it One on
the Anglican theory ?   Is it not repugnant to common
sense to say that there is *unity* between Rome and
the so-called Greek Church and Anglicanism ?   Yet

unity, and unity of the strictest kind, is the unity of the Church of Christ (St. John xvii.). Unity! why what is the sign of Church unity?—is it not the Communion of the Blessed Sacrament? And where is this to be found between any of these three bodies? Why! the Catholic denies that Anglican ministers are Priests, and no Catholic would receive the bread and wine from an Anglican Minister's hand; the Anglican presumes to affirm on his principle of corporate reunion that the Catholic Church, though Catholic at Boulogne, is schismatical at Dover, and he could not consistently join in schismatical Communion, though he knows that the Body of the Lord is consecrated by a Catholic Priest and he cannot be quite sure (*we* know he has no right to be sure at all) that Anglican Ministers have any power to consecrate. There is no unity between the Catholic Church and Anglicanism, and there cannot be as long as each remains what it is and so long as union is sought without the intention of admitting the divine institution of a visible Head. And, indeed, the common sense of Englishmen is finding out that the Catholic Church and the Anglican body cannot be both true Churches—that if one is true, the other is false; and Englishmen are beginning to prefer certainty in the possession of the sacraments with the one to special pleading for the other.

But to teach truth is another characteristic of Christ's Church, and here again we must appeal to common sense in its judgment of facts. I cannot resist here putting the simple question to a partisan of the corporate reunion theory, "Do you really wish—do you believe that it would be to the greater glory of

C 2

God—that the Anglican Bishops should be received
on equal terms with the Bishops of the Catholic
Church ?   Do you really believe that the Church
would be helped to fulfil her duty of teaching the
truth by the union of the so-called Bishops of London,
Hereford, Natal, Winchester, Bangor, and St. David's,
with the Bishops of the Catholic Church in Belgium,
France, and Italy?   I do not think that you would
wish it for the advantage of truth."   But yet, if the
Catholic Church and the Anglican body are both
possessed of the essentials of a Church, it follows that
they both teach the truth which has been committed
to the Church's keeping.   Now common sense must
confess that Anglicans—that is, the various Anglican
dioceses under their respective Bishops — do not by
any means hold the same doctrines as the Catholic
Bishops.   It is in vain to appeal to the High Church
Anglicans, they are but a section, and, compared with
the so-called Evangelical school and the so-called
Liberal school, only a *small* section of the Anglican
body.   So we have in Anglicanism itself at least three
opposing schools which denounce each other as not
teaching truth in essential matters ; and then there is
the Catholic Church in England teaching, in opposition
to them all, the absolute necessity of the recognition
of the visible Head of the Church.   Surely, surely,
common honesty must allow that if these are both of
them true Churches, the truth which Christ delivered
to be taught is self-contradictory ; but since that truth
cannot be self-contradictory, most certainly these two
are not both of them true Churches, one must be a
false Church and a pretender, and restoration of unity

by corporate reunion must be regarded as an *ignus fatuus*, effective indeed too often to keep back earnest inquirers from joining their true Mother—the true Church of their Baptism—but keeping them back by a delusion.

As then, both *à priori*—and from the credentials of the Church, the words of her Founder in Holy Scripture—and from the evidence of facts, it is plain that the recognition of a visible Head of the Church is a matter essential to the being of *the* Church, and of *a* Church, may you who already confess this truth cling to it as part of God's gift to man; and you who are longing for peace in believing, enter the one fold of the Catholic Church under its one Shepherd— Jesus Christ being the Chief Pastor of the Church visible and invisible, and His Vicar upon earth being His visible representative over the visible portion of His Church, the Kingdom of Heaven upon earth.

LECTURE III.

THE SINS OF CHRISTIANS.

The Kingdom of Heaven is like to a net cast into the sea, and gathering together of all kinds of fishes.—St. Matt. xiii. 47.

WHEN Anglicans are urged by Catholics to give up their system as being inconsistent with the unity of the Church which is taught in Holy Scripture and the Creeds, one of two answers is generally given. Some are bold enough to assert that, notwithstanding their differences, the Roman, the Greek, and the Anglican bodies are still substantially one, because they all have the Apostolic succession, and all teach essential truth. This bold assertion was disproved last Sunday, and it was shown that different bodies like the Catholic Church and the Anglican Establishment can in no sense be called one, and that finely-spun theories must give way to common sense. They are not one—it is contrary to common sense to assert that they are; they are not one, it is contrary to common honesty to pretend that they are. As to Apostolical succession, its possession, were it real, would argue no more for Anglicans than for Donatists. As to the teaching, two bodies at issue on the fundamental question—*What are fundamentals?* —cannot be two real branches of the truth-teaching Church, and it is a fact that Anglicans deny, while Roman Catholics affirm, that the question about the necessity of union with the Apostolic See is a funda-mental one. Both these bodies then cannot be true Churches; one or the other must be a pretender, and those who find themselves in the pretender must, with-out waiting for others, seek their safety in the true ark of salvation.

Others, beaten from this entrenchment, take refuge in another. They declare it is a mournful fact that the Church is indeed no longer one; that God intended it to be one, that Holy Scripture exhibits it as one, that the Creeds call it one, but that, though once it was one, it is now divided, and that the account of its being divided is the sin of men, which has marred the beauty of God's work, and spoiled it, and broken into frag-ments the perfect fabric which once existed. They say that this is only one instance out of many in which God's fairest works have been frustrated, and that it is the sin of man that has entailed this disappointment.

Wonderful infatuation! Why the sin of men, so far from destroying the unity of the Church, is the very thing that renders the unity necessary, and the greater the sin of men and of Christians, the more necessary is it that the Church which was instituted to carry out the work of redemption should be clearly, distinctly, actually one. Strange doctrine indeed to say that a malady changes the character of the remedy intended to correct it. Does ague change the qualities of Peruvian bark, or because the ague increases in intensity, does it destroy the qualities of that remedy, or render its use less necessary? True indeed it is that sin mars God's work, and it has marred God's work even in the Church which He has purchased with His own Blood;

sin has marred it in the corruption of too many of its members, and every mortal sin committed by a Catholic is a sad proof how men's evil will can disappoint God's goodness, but the existence of this evil in the Church, without interfering with her unity, has been foretold from the beginning, for our Blessed Lord Himself has compared His Church to a field in which the enemy sows tares with the wheat; to a net in which fish are taken, both bad and good; to the ten virgins, five of whom were wise and five foolish; to a marriage feast where was found a guest not having the wedding garment. Sin too has marred God's gracious designs in the spirit of misbelief as to divine truth, and rebellion as to divinely-established authority; but it has been not in dividing the Church so that it should exist in the disunion of separate independent Churches, but in separating from the Body the mortified limb, and cutting off from the trunk the fruitless branches; by the fall of the East into schism, and of the Anglican Establishment into schism and many a grievous heresy.

However, it may be worth while to consider more in detail this defence made by Anglicans of their isolated position. Sin, *they* say, has forfeited this gift to the Church of God; sin, *we* say, is the very thing that renders the permanence of this gift more necessary.

Our Lord God, in His dealings with individuals and nations, uses promises and threats. He threatens the forfeiture of the blessings He bestows as the punishment for sin, and He promises blessings and rewards to those who fulfil His holy will. His threats are, we may say, always conditional; His promises often are conditional, but not always, for there are circumstances in which His promises are unconditional, and the promise that the gates of hell shall not prevail against His Church is of this kind, unconditional, as will easily appear. God's denunciations are conditional; He threatens punishment to the wicked, but it is contrary to His wish to punish and take vengeance. The very threats that He uses are made in mercy; by His holding out the terrors of His punishments, He desires to terrify the sinner into wisdom. Therefore it is that our Blessed Lord opens before us the terrors of hell, that he speaks of the worm that does not die, of the fire that is not extinguished; that, if our love for God fail us, at least our fear of Him and of His just judgments may scare us from iniquity. "As I live," saith the Lord God, "I desire not the death of the wicked, but that the wicked turn from his ways and live. Turn ye, turn ye from your evil ways. And why will you die, O house of Israel? If I shall say to the wicked, Thou shalt surely die; and if he do penance for his sin, and do judgment and justice, and if that wicked man restore the pledge, and render what he had robbed, and walk in the commandments of life, and do no unjust thing, he shall surely live and not die. None of his sins which he hath committed shall be imputed unto him : he hath done judgment and justice, and he shall surely live " (Ezech. xxxiii. 14).

This truth, which we all feel to be unquestionable, is confirmed by examples in Holy Scripture. It is said of King Achab that there was not such another as Achab, who was sold to do evil in the sight of the Lord, and he became abominable, insomuch that he worshipped the idols of the Ammonites; and yet, when he had heard the denunciations of the Prophet Elias, that God would bring evil upon him and his posterity, he rent his garments, and put hair-cloth upon his flesh, and fasted, and slept in sackcloth, and walked with his head cast down. And the result was that the word of the Lord came to Elias — "Hast thou not seen Achab humbled before me? therefore, because he hath humbled himself for My sake, I will not bring the evil in his days, but in his son's days I will bring the evil upon his house" (3 Kings xxi. 25—29). Again, Jonas, in the reign of Jeroboam the Second, was sent by the Lord to Nineveh, because the wickedness of the city came up before. Him, and he preached at God's bidding, "Yet forty days and Nineveh shall be destroyed." And the Ninevites did penance, from the greatest to the least, and God had mercy with regard to the evil which He had said that He would do to them, and He did it not. And Jonas said he knew "He was a gracious and merciful God; patient and of much compassion, and easy to forgive evil" (Jonas iv. 2).

But there needs little to prove God's willingness to forgive; little to show that his threats are conditional, and that contrition and repentance can disarm the anger of God. His promises, what are they?—are they also conditional, and, if they are in some cases, are there others in which they are unconditional? It may easily be seen that some are conditional and some are not, and examples will illustrate the distinction between the two. Promises are conditional when their effect is confined to the person or nation to whom the promise is made; promises are unconditional when their fulfilment involves the interests of others.

The promise, then, of reward, in which no interest but that of the person to whom the promise is made is concerned, will be conditional. "Do this and thou shalt live." The promise of life is made contingent on fidelity to the commandments of God, and disobedience would forfeit the promise. Saul was chosen to be King of Israel, but he disobeyed the word of the Lord through Samuel, and, forasmuch as he had rejected the word of the Lord, the Lord also rejected him from being King. To Judas Iscariot was made the promise that he should sit on a throne judging the tribes of Israel, but Judas by transgression fell.

But where the promise involved the interest of others, its fulfilment might easily become unconditional and might necessarily be so; and so far from sin forfeiting the promise it might render its fulfilment still more necessary. Take the promise of a Redeemer. Here the salvation of a whole world was concerned, and the promise is made that the seed of the woman should bruise the serpent's head and destroy the works of the devil. Here is a promise that is unconditional, and so far from the sins of men depriving that promise of its effect, the deeper the world sank in iniquity the more necessary became the Saviour, and the more desirous was God of showing His mercy. And not only was the promise of a Saviour unconditional, but— which, however, is not necessary to the argument—the promise that the Saviour should spring from a particular family was, in fact, to all appearance unconditional too. The members of that family might by their sins forfeit their share in the blessing of redemption, but still their sin did not make the promise of God of no effect, either

with regard to the general promise of a Saviour, or
(which might have been without weakening the argument) to the particular promise that, He should spring
from a particular nation, because in this the interests of
the world were concerned, and their iniquity would
reach only themselves.   Hence, notwithstanding the
sins of the Hebrews, of the house of Judah, of the sons
of David, "Salvation," as our Blessed Lord said to the
woman of Samaria, "was of the Jews" (St. John iv. 22),
and Messiah was born of a Virgin of the stock and
lineage of David.

Of a piece with this is the known fact that the effect
of the sacraments does not depend on the holiness of
the person who administers them.   "Whose sins you
shall forgive they are forgiven them, and whose sins you
shall retain they are retained," is a promise made for
the benefit of all Christians, as it that other—"Is any
man sick among you? let him bring in the Priests of
the Church, and let them pray over him, anointing him
with oil in the name of the Lord ; and if he be in sins
they shall be forgiven him."   Whatever be the imper-
fections of the Minister of Christ, the promise is sure
and the blessing of forgiveness is conveyed.

So is it with the Church of Jesus Christ as a visible
body, as the perpetuation, in some sense, of the Incar-
nation, inasmuch as the Church was founded and is
continued in order to perpetuate the work which Jesus
Christ Himself began while visibly on earth.   It is a
City set upon a hill, the City of God, the City of
Refuge, built by Jesus Christ for those who feel their
need of forgiveness, of knowledge and of the grace of
God. The very fact of the sinfulness of the world was

a reason why this City should be set on high, visible
and one; and the sins of men, whether within or
without the Church, do not diminish but perpetuate
the necessity of the City of Refuge being still set on
high, visible and one.

Such being the case, it ought to be felt by Anglicans that the *absolute promise* of unity, coupled with
the *doubt* which the rest of Christendom throws on
their Orders, determines that this unity is not on the
side of Anglicanism. The promise of unity is unconditional; hence Anglicanism and the Catholic Church
cannot be both true Churches, one must be a pretender.
Now Anglicans grant that the Roman Catholic Church
is a true Church, but Catholics do not allow this of the
Anglican Establishment. Anglicans grant that we have
true Orders and true sacraments; they affirm the same
of themselves, but the rest of Christendom denies it.
Anglicans confess that in the Holy Mass is true consecration; it is by us denied that they have true
consecration; and were it only that our Blessed Lord's
Body might not be exposed to so many sacrileges from
the immense majority of Anglicans having no idea of
the Real Presence, even Anglicans themselves ought
hardly to regret the invalidity of consecration in the
Anglican Communion service. On the side of the
Roman Catholic Church there is undisputed certainty;
on their side there *must be*, at least, doubt. Since, then,
one or other must be denied to be the true Church, on
which side must common sense and prudence decide?

But has sin no disastrous effects as regards the
Church? It is not hard to discern the effects of sin,
whether we consider sin outside the Church or within

it. In both cases the necessity of the Church's unity is demonstrated.

There was and is sin outside the Church. It was to destroy the works of the devil that our Blessed Lord Jesus Christ came and taught and died ; it was for this same purpose that the Church was instituted and exists. There has been war waged against the Church all along. The world, the concupiscences, and the Prince of darkness, have been leagued against her. Philosophy, Alexandrian and Oriental ; idolatry, Roman and Greek, Syrian and Egyptian ; force and violence, imperial and popular, have waged unremitting war against the Church, at its birth, as it grew, and through its duration. What has been the effect of sin outside the Church—division ? No ; but consolidation. The gates of hell have not prevailed against it. But it is said that all question of sin outside the Church is waived, and it is asked what is the effect of sin within the Church. The answer is ready. It is *not* such as to interfere with the unity of the Church. The parables of our Lord descriptive of the Church make this evident. In the field where tares were sown and mixed with the wheat, both were allowed to grow together till the harvest ; in the vine, the unfruitful branches are cut off, but the vine itself continues one ; in the net good and bad fishes are taken, but the bad fishes do not cause the net to break. So in the City set on a hill, based on Jesus Christ the Rock, and on Peter, whose name indicates his privilege, there have been and there will be scandals, but it is not written, "Woe to the Church of God because of scandals," but, "Woe to the man by whom the scandal comes ;" as it was not said, "Woe to the Apostolic Choir," because Judas was one of the Apostles, but "Woe to Júdas."

There may be sins of two kinds, and the parables just referred to indicate the different way in which transgressors in either kind are treated. There may be offenders against the moral law of the Church, and there may be offenders against her authority. The former are not rebels any more than the drunkard or thief is guilty of high treason ; in the latter, not only does obedience fail but the right of exacting it is denied. The former are like the tares which are allowed to remain till the harvest ; the latter must be cut off like the unfruitful branches of the vine. Some of these latter may deny the right of the Church to teach, and so are guilty of heresy ; others may deny the right of the Church to govern them, and so are guilty of schism. These, so long as they are obstinate, cannot be regarded by the Church as her faithful subjects, and they must be cut off ; and this may be the only chance of their being brought to repentance, or, at any rate, in this way only the leaven of their example may be prevented from spreading among the rest of the community. Moral faults, then, may exist in members of the Church and do not effect her unity ; schism and heresy involve expulsion from the Church, and though they do not effect her unity, they entail the separation of the guilty from that unity. They are cut off, while the Church herself remains intact—as a diseased limb is cut off and dies, while the body retains the principle of life and lives.

The sins, therefore, of Christians cannot be regarded as a cause on account of which the Church, established

by Christ in unity, has been suffered to fall into disunion.   And who are the inventors of this strange
doctrine ?   They whose turn it serves.   They are, in
fact, cut off from the unity of Christendom, and they
must needs excuse themselves ; they are in schism,
and they must find some plea for their schism. Rather
than strike their breasts and say, "We have sinned,"
and return to the unity of the Body of Christ, they
will set aside the clearest evidence of Holy Scripture
to the necessary unity of the Church, and assert that
the seamless robe of Christ has been rent into three
parts, and allow that there no longer exists on earth
a sure and certain means of condemning heresies when
they arise or of determining dogmatic truth.

Meantime, the true Church of Christ looks on and
waits God's time, and many, wearied out with the
uncertainties and shifts of Anglicanism, are seeking
truth in her bosom.   May the Holy Spirit of God
multiply their numbers, and restore, not unity to the
Church, for she cannot lose it, but restore them to the
Church's unity.

LECTURE IV. ·

ROME'S CLAIM.

Korah, Dathan, and Abiron, stood up against Moses and Aaron, and said, Let it be enough for you that all the multitude consisteth of holy ones and the Lord is among them? Why lift you up yourselves above the people of the Lord?—Numbers xvi. 1—3.

A PARENT who failed to maintain his parental authority would prove false to a trust committed to him by Almighty God. Such authority is given for the good of the children, and the exercise of it is an exercise of charity. It cannot be neglected without transgression of God's law, for the commandment enjoining the honour to be paid to parents is reciprocal, and it imposes upon parents the responsibility of exercising aright the parental authority, no less than. it imposes on children the duty of obedience. Even when the parent punishes, his just severity is an exercise of charity, for "What son is there whom the father doth not correct?" If, then, the children of a family were to upbraid their parents with pride and arrogance because the latter faithfully discharged their duty and required filial obedience, it would be against the children that the charge of pride and arrogance would fairly lie, and not against the parents. Moses and Aaron were set in authority by God over the people of Israel. Korah, Dathan, and Abiron, on the plea that all the people were holy as chosen by God, and that God

D

Himself was among them, and therefore needed no
representatives like Moses and Aaron, resisted the
authority of God's representatives and perished miser-
ably by a divine sentence.

As in the preceding lecture we examined the argument by which it is pretended that the Church is no
longer visibly One in punishment for the sins of
Christians in general, and we showed that the promise
of unity to the Church was unconditional and that the
existence of sin only renders more necessary the unity
of the Church ; so to-day let us consider a particular
sin which is constantly urged by Anglicans against
the Holy See, and pleaded in defence of separation
from it. They charge the Holy Father with pride and
arrogance. His claim to be the visible Head of the
Church is, they say, an arrogant pretence, a claim to
domineer over the Church of Christ, and was the cause,
in the first instance, of the separation between the
Western and the Eastern Churches, and, in later times,
of the separation between the See of Rome and
Anglicanism.

Strange sophistry by which these men dissuade
others from seeking peace and grace and truth from
the fountains of the sacraments of the true Church
of Christ ! Strange sophistry and judicial blindness !
As though this charge of arrogancy against the successor of St. Peter for claiming the visible Headship
of the visible Church were not a simple *petitio principii*,
a "begging the question," and a taking for granted
that which ought to be proved, namely, that they are
justified in their separation. The very question is,
whether or not our Blessed Lord appointed St. Peter

and his successors as the Chief Pastors of the Church.
If he did not, then indeed their claim would be arrogant,
and there would be a reason for separation ; if he did,
the claim is not arrogant, there is no "proud lording
it over the Clergy" or domineering over the Faithful,
but only the performance of a bounden duty, the
exercise of an unenviable, because so serious, a responsibility.

The proof that our Blessed Lord did actually
establish the divine government of His Church under
Bishops bound into unity by a visible Head, was given
in the second lecture. Here I will briefly state the
argument. Of course the real ground for admitting
this constitution is that God Himself proposes it to
us through His Church ; but besides this, we argue
that as our Blessed Lord constituted His Church, and
as it existed in the time of the Apostles, so it was to
continue to the end of the world. Now, in those times
it was governed essentially by an Episcopate and Priesthood, with a special commission given to St. Peter to
govern the whole flock. As then the Episcopate and
the Priesthood are perpetuated, so is the visible Headship ; and if we have regard to the words used by our
Blessed Lord, the expressions used by Him with regard
to the commission bestowed on St. Peter are extra-
ordinarily emphatic, distinct, and reiterated. Thus
much is of divine institution ; the fact of St. Peter's
successors being Bishops of Rome is matter of incon-
testable history. So far as the divine institution is
concerned they might have been Bishops of any other
see ; but long before he went to Rome, St. Peter had
received his authority, just before the Ascension of our

D 2

Lord. When he arrived in Rome and made it his see,
he retained his authority, and the other Churches, elder
it may be to Rome, but not elder to the divine commission given to St. Peter, continued subject to St.
Peter and his successors, and became subject to the
Bishop of Rome as being St. Peter's successor.

Here, by the way, may be noticed a trivial objection
urged by Anglican controversialists. They ask, " How
should Canterbury be subject to Rome? There is
reason, they say, to believe that the Church of Britain
is as old, or older, than the Church of Rome. How
then can it be required of her to recognise the
supremacy of Rome, to say nothing of Jerusalem and
Antioch, which certainly were Churches more ancient
than Rome?" The more a man studies the difficulties
urged by non-Catholics against the Church, the more
trivial and childish do the arguments of their learned
men appear. What Catholic ever urged obedience to
the Holy See because it so happens that it is fixed
at Rome? The obligation of obedience is not to the
Bishop of Rome as such, but to St. Peter and his
successors; and it would be difficult to prove that
either the Church of Canterbury, or of Jerusalem, or
of Antioch, was older than the date of St. Peter's
prerogative—"Thou art Peter, and on this rock I will
build My Church;" "Feed My lambs, feed My sheep;"
" To thee I will give the *keys* (the symbol of authority)
of the Kingdom of Heaven."

St. Peter, then, having received, and his successors
having inherited, the government of the whole flock,
we have not to go far to form a judgment how God
will regard those who treat this commission lightly,

or accuse its exercise of arrogance. No doubt Ozias
(2 Par. xxvi. 16) thought Azarias the Priest arrogant,
when he resisted his royal person on his daring to
burn incense in the sanctuary and usurping the prerogative of the sons of Aaron ; and he threatened the
Priests, but presently he felt the stroke of the Lord,
and the leprosy appeared on his forehead. We are
told that this charge of arrogance and domineering
was brought against Moses and Aaron by Korah,
Dathan, and Abiron. "Let it be enough for you,"
they said, "that all the multitude consisteth of holy
ones, and the Lord is among them. Why lift you up
yourselves against the people of the Lord ?" Korah
and his followers would not tolerate the idea of a
r epresentative of God ; they had God Himself among
them, and they called it arrogance for Moses and
Aaron to claim the superiority. But this superiority
was a grave commission intrusted to Moses and Aaron
by God, and Moses and Aaron could not without
offence to God fail to exact its recognition ; and the
judgment of God on the accusers proved that the
arrogance was on the side, not of the divinely-appointed
chiefs, but of the murmuring subjects.

"If they have called the Master Beelzebub, how
much more those of His household" (St. Matt. x. 25).
It was thought arrogance in our Blessed Lord to set
Himself up as the Son of God, greater than Solomon,
the Chastiser of the Scribes and Pharisees, and the
Avenger of His Father's and the Temple's honour.
It is only remoteness of time that prevents the charge
of arrogance against St. Paul because he delivered up
Hymenæus and Philetus to Satan, that they might

learn not to blaspheme; or against St. Peter when he presumed to pronounce sentence, confirmed by miracle, on Ananias and Sapphira, for lying against the Holy Ghost. However, notwithstanding the charge of arrogance, men placed in offices of trust by God are bound to fulfil this trust, and, as necessary to that fulfilment, to exact its recognition when need requires. Neglect of such responsibility is culpable, and is visited with punishment. Of this, Heli the High-Priest is an example. The scandalous behaviour of his sons drew down punishment on him, because, as God said to Samuel, "He knew that his sons did wickedly, and did not chasten them."

What, then, assuming the divine commission given to St. Peter to watch over the whole Church, might we naturally expect would be the facts of history? We might be sure that they who loved the Church would prove faithful to its appointed Head, as the institution of Christ and the guarantee of unity; and no less we might expect that there would arise men like Koran, Dathan, and Abiron, who should dispute the authority of the visible Head and charge him with arrogancy. License of speculation in matters of doctrine, impatience of authority in matters of practice, would be, both of them, rife with occasions of discontent, and if the visible Head exercised his authority in suppressing dangerous speculations, or in vindicating the visible Headship which is necessary to the unity of the Church, he would be accused of arrogancy and pride.

So long as there was no need to exert the authority given to St. Peter and his successors, it would exist without being shown, for real divine authority needs no parade. St. Peter would be as a brother among the rest of the Apostles, and, as they were all secured by the Holy Ghost in matters of faith no less than himself, there might be perhaps no occasion for him personally to exert the gift for which Jesus Christ had prayed—"I have prayed for thee that thy faith fail not, and do thou, in turn, confirm thy brethren." It might be that the faith delivered to the immediate successors of the Apostles would have been held so firmly by the vast majority that any exceptional cases of error-teaching Bishops would be sufficiently guarded against by the predominant orthodoxy of their surrounding brethren (Acts xxviii. 28). In that case, appeals to Metropolitans, or Councils, or Patriarchs— and, much more, the ultimate appeal to the Church in Council assembled, with St. Peter's successor at the head—would have been unnecessary. Bishops might decide differences in their own dioceses, erring Bishops might be judged by their Metropolitans, at the worst an appeal might be made to a Patriarch; but till Patriarchs themselves failed in their duty, the authority of the visible Head might only exist, and not be exerted. However, in *fact*, causes in which Bishops were concerned were soon reserved to the See of Rome, as appears evident (A.D. 342) in the Letter of Pope Julius to the Oriental Bishops who had condemned some of their colleagues. "Know you not that the custom is that *we* should be first written to, and that *here* [at Rome] should be decided what is right? . . . I merely state that which we have received from the blessed Apostle Peter, and I should not have written it—believing it to be known to the whole world—had not the attempts which have been made thrown us into amazement."

It would be, *à priori*, perfectly *conceivable* that no real occasion for the exercise of the authority given to Peter and his successors might occur for hundreds of years. And yet that authority would really exist, not asleep but not parading itself; ready for an emergency when the Church's need required it, but making no show so long as its energy was not wanted, and whatever plausibility there is in the often-repeated assertion (an assertion as remarkable for its untruthfulness as for its effrontery) that for six hundred years the claim of the primacy of St. Peter's successor was unheard of, it is derived entirely from the comparative non-necessity of its actual exercise. And yet occasions did occur for its exercise, and in these it manifested itself. The See of St. Peter was, indeed, as careful not to interfere with the rightful jurisdiction of Bishops as it was to set them right when they went wrong. It would not take cognisance of the cause of a heretic (Marcion) rightly condemned by his own Bishop, while it extended its protection over the whole Christian world when orthodox Bishops were assailed and exiled (as St. Athanasius), or Bishops taught error (as Firmilian), or Patriarchs (as Nestorius). It urged Catholic uniformity in the observance of Easter in Asia, though it tempered its zeal when the prudence of a counsellor (St. Irenæus) recommended its not proceeding to extremities. Christians in proportion to their orthodoxy were devoted to the See of St. Peter. If their orthodoxy declined they were estranged ; if their orthodoxy were lost they rebelled.

Hence Tertullian, when fallen into heresy, ridiculed the Chief Pastor who claimed to be Bishop of Bishops; and St. Cyprian when he maintained the material heresy of Anabaptism, in opposition to St. Stephen, seemed to lose sight of his former loyalty to the Holy See, and adopted language which was unbecoming. And yet Anglicans who confess that St. Stephen was right and St. Cyprian was wrong as to this (now) article of faith, seem to forget that the Pope, as it were, single-handed, maintained the faith which themselves profess against the Bishops of Asia Minor and Africa, and that on his firmness, humanly speaking, the Catholic faith depended for its perpetuity. Thanks to the "domineering arrogance" of St. Stephen, the heresy of the Anabaptists did not become the doctrine of Christendom.

As to blessed St. Cyprian, it was his conviction of the absolute necessity of actual unity that saved him from being carried away by material heresy into schism, and his glorious martyrdom, just after that of Pope St. Xystus, the successor of St. Stephen, makes us willingly forget—did not the sophistry of others render it necessary to explain his conduct—his unadvised words, if they are genuine, in the Anabaptist controversy.*

The various Councils of the early centuries treat of the authority of Bishops, Metropolitans, and Patriarchs as

---

* St. Stephen was martyred A.D. 257, and was succeeded by Xystus II. St. Xystus II. martyred A.D. 258, August 6 (*Ep.* lxxxii. *S. Cyprian*). St. Cyprian martyred A.D. 258, September 14. St. Xystus wrote conciliatory letters to the Churches of Africa and Cappadocia, Galatia, and Cilicia. These must have arrived before St. Cyprian's martyrdom, as appears from the above dates. St. Xystus is called *Bonus et pacificus sacerdos* by Pontius, Deacon and biographer of St. Cyprian, which implies that there had ensued *peace* between the Bishop of Rome and St. Cyprian during the Pontificate of St. Xystus, the successor of St. Stephen.

such. The exceptional cases of the interference of the
Holy See do not call for such frequent mention, yet,
when there is a question of an ultimate appeal, it is
taken for granted that the appeal is to St. Peter's
successor in the See of Rome. This is plain from the
Councils of Nicæa, Sardica, Ephesus, and Chalcedon,
three of which were Œcumenical Councils, and are so
regarded by Anglicans; and in them the recognition
of the authority of the Holy See is made by the
assembled Bishops of the Eastern Church.

And then comes the trivial charge of arrogance
again, as though the Bishop of Rome claimed an
authority disclaimed by St. Gregory. The argument
is this: "Pope St. Gregory condemned as arrogant
the assumption by John, Bishop of Constantinople, of
the title of *Universal Bishop;* therefore it is arrogant in
the Pope to allow himself to be so entitled, or to claim
that title now." How is the Holy See cleared of the
charge of arrogance? The title *Universal Bishop* is
capable of two meanings. It would be arrogant to
claim that title in one of those meanings; the title
certainly belongs to St. Peter's successor in the other.
Let it be remarked that the visible Headship of the
Church is not like that of a King over his kingdom;
to affirm that the relation of the Chief Pastor to the
Bishops of the Church is that of a King over his
Viceroys would be false,* for Viceroys and officers

* "To speak properly, the Pope as such is no monarch (as regards the
Church) at all, much less the universal one. The reason is because the
word monarch is properly taken for one to whom all others placed in
authority are but as Vicars, Deputies, or Vice-Regents. In which sense
Christ is the only universal Monarch both of the world and of the Church;
for all Bishops are His Vicars, and all Princes His Vice-Regents, and this
cannot be attributed to the Pope" (*Manning's Answer to Lesley*). Indeed,

appointed by the King are merely his deputies, and can at his will be deprived of their character. If, then, the title "Universal Bishop" signifies power of this kind, none but our Lord Jesus Christ Himself has any right to it, for His deputies are at once the Chief Pastor and the rest of the Bishops. But the Bishops of the Church are not the deputies of St. Peter and of his successors. St. Gregory, believing that this title assumed by John of Constantinople implied this error, condemned it, for, he argued, if any were Universal Bishop in this sense, in case he fell, all the other Bishops, being merely his deputies, would fall too, and so the whole Church would fall. But as certainly as St. Gregory condemned the title Universal Bishop in the sense which implied that all other Bishops were merely his deputies, so most certainly he maintained, as in duty bound, the *fact* that the Holy See was the Head of all Churches, and that the Bishop of that See was the Head to whom the care and primacy of the whole Church was committed. The question of St. Gregory's conflict with John of Constantinople is a question about the meaning of a word ; the *fact* of the primacy of St. Peter's successor St. Gregory maintained. If the objectionable meaning be excluded from the use of the word "Universal Bishop," if it be used to express only the possession of the Headship of the Church, while all the other Bishops really possess—not as mere deputies,

when a Bishop is consecrated, He receives the Episcopal character in its integrity (*in solidum*), and is by no means a mere deputy of the visible Head ; he is as much Bishop as the Pope himself—as a Priest is as much Priest as the Pope himself, and it would be as impossible for the visible Head to suppress all the Bishoprics in Christendom as to destroy anything else in the Church which is of divine right, or to teach that virtue is to be shunned and vice to be practised.

but as divinely-ordained Pastors of the Church of God
—the Episcopal character in its integrity, then the use
of that title becomes no longer objectionable, and the
same Chief Pastor of the Church on earth may be called,
by virtue of his prerogative, the Universal Bishop, and,
in his humility, servant of the servants of God.

Finally, let our Anglican fellow-countrymen only
use their common sense, and look at Catholics through
the world.   Let them look at us English Catholics.
Are we groaning under a tyranny which oppresses us
and hampers us?   Do we shrink and flinch from
Pius IX., our Head in point of fact, and their Head,
too, in point of right, as though he exercised a power
over us which degraded us and paralysed us ? If they
imagine that it is so, we can only assure them of the
contrary, and declare that the fatherly love of our
spiritual Head is an easy yoke and a light burden—
as Jesus Christ said Himself: "Take My yoke upon
you ; My yoke is easy and My burden is light." It is
so light we do not feel it. We rejoice in it because
it is our safeguard against error, and our security from
the numberless delusions of the human reason when it
goes out of its sphere and speculates rashly on super-
natural truth.   The successor of St. Peter was always,
in old time, as Anglicans themselves allow, on the right
side in matters of faith, and now our Anglican friends
will never escape the quicksands of ever-shifting opinion
till they return to the Rock which is Christ by divine
right ; and the warrant of their being on that Rock is
their being built on Peter and his successors, who are
the visible Rock by divine commission.

LECTURE V.

The Kingdom of Heaven is like to a merchant seeking good pearls, who when he had found one pearl of great price, went his way and sold all that he had and bought it.—St. Matt. xiii. 45, 46.

THE salvation of our souls is a personal matter; we may not wait for others when our salvation is at stake. " Je mourrai seul," was the expression of an eminent man. I shall be alone when I die, I shall be alone when I am judged ; my sentence for good or evil will be personal, and it will be useless to plead that in my sin or in my schism I was associated with many others. If any could have had a right to wait for others, to wait until there should be a corporate union with the Christian Church, it would have been the Jews, for their religion certainly was divine, and individuals might with seeming reason have said that the Old Covenant must naturally blossom into the New, and that individuals might wait for the entire body. But no ! this was not Christ's way ; he called men, one here, another there. It was by the conversion of individuals the Church was spread ; and had men waited till all Israel had been ready to believe, there would not in this nineteenth century have existed the Christian Church. Every intimation of Holy Scripture refers to the Church as visibly one ; the parables of our Lord, and the comparisons he uses—a sheepfold, a kingdom, the human body, declare her to be one ; one by a unity inconsistent with severance into independent parts, but not inconsistent with the presence of scandals and of sinners, for the field contained wheat and tares, which were allowed to grow together till the harvest, and the drag-net contained all kinds of fishes, good and bad, but without breaking.

The opinion that every Bishop with his local flock is so fully possessed of the essentials of a Church as to retain the integrity of a Church, even though unhappily separated from a centre of unity divinely appointed, is an opinion which has gained a footing only among those whose position has rendered it necessary to look about for an excuse for schism. At a time when, without prejudice, the notes of the Church were enumerated, all Christians agreed in professing their faith in *One* Holy Catholic and Apostolic Church, and we feel it to be contrary to common sense to imagine that they could ever have supposed that this unity should have been consistent with the state of the Church as pretended by Anglicans in these days ; made up, as they say, of three independent branches, un-united in a common stock, not intercommunicating with each other, and teaching contradictorily as to the fundamental question, *What is fundamental ?*

There is a hidden cancer in this system which robs it of all soundness ; it is the false and worldly principle of *independency.* Here is an application to independent Churches of that principle which, applied to individual congregations, has resulted in what is called among Dissenters, independency; it applies to Bishops what by Independents is applied to laymen. Dissenters and Independents dispense with the divine institution of Priests and Bishops; the ritualistic advocates of corporate reunion dispense with the divine institution of the visible Head and centre of unity. But the commission given to St. Peter is as express as that given to the Episcopate—the Episcopate and its visible Head stand or fall together. And the history of the world is plainly indicating that between Catholicity and individual independence there is no standing-place; the principle of dissolution will dissolve unless the principle of unity is possessed, and it will be patent soon to all that there can be no Church without Peter, in the full sense of St. Ambrose's words, *Ubi Petrus, ubi Ecclesia*—where Peter is, and there only, is the Church.

It will be useful to make some practical observations on the matter-of-fact impossibility of the corporate reunion advocated by High Church Anglicans. It is impossible *now*, and there is no *prospect* of it becoming possible; it is impossible now, whether you regard the *Catholic Church* itself, or the separated *Anglicans;* it is impossible, as well on grounds of doctrinal teaching as of the question of Orders. Some remarks shall be made on these several points.

This corporate reunion is impossible if you regard the Catholic Church; for it is not pretended that the reunion could take place without concessions on the part of the Catholic Church, and these concessions are, as I will show, impossible.

First of all, let it be remarked that there is not a Catholic theologian in the whole world who does not teach and regard as essential doctrine that union with

the successor of St. Peter is absolutely necessary to
the being of a Church. This is doctrine contained in
the catechisms of the child, and not a question disputed
in the schools.   Before, then, the advocates of corporate
reunion can hope ever to be admitted into court to
demand concessions, they must persuade all the Catholic
Bishops, Priests, theologians, and laymen throughout
the world that this is an error; for unless this be an
error, Anglicanism can never be admitted as having
rights to maintain, or a claim to concessions.   Now
this is impossible, and this impossibility shows that it
is not in this way that the Anglican body is to recover
unity.   It may be said, "It is equally impossible to
persuade all the teachers and taught of the Anglican
Establishment of the absolute necessity of union with
St. Peter's See."   And so it may be, and from this
follows again the impossibility of corporate reunion, and
consequently the necessity of individual conversions to
Catholicity, since after all both Catholics and Anglicans
confess the Church in union with St. Peter's See to be
a true Church, while Anglicans alone try to persuade
themselves of the Churchship of Anglicanism.

      It has been said that while individuals can obtain
little from Rome, bodies of men may obtain much, and
the examples are quoted of united Greeks, the Arme-
nians, and the Maronites.   The Maronites of Mount
Libanus, in the sixteenth century, obtained, it is said,
"The use of the chalice, and the marriage of Priests,
and the use of their own language in the Divine Office.
Why should not the Anglicans make the same terms
and obtain them?"   I answer, for the very best of
reasons, and since time will not allow our entering on

all the cases mentioned, I will speak of one, since the
principle which applies to that one is applicable to all.

It is said, the Maronites are allowed by the Church
of Rome Communion under both kinds, why should not
Anglicans obtain this concession ? I answer, because
Anglicans demand this on principles of heresy, and the
Maronites possessed it by time-honoured tradition ; and
I explain my meaning : Communion, under one or both
kinds, is mere matter of discipline, and has varied
according to circumstances in the history of the Church.
A simple comparison will make this plain. Under no
circumstances could the Church have used wine in
baptising, because water is matter of necessity, and not
of mere discipline ; since therefore the primitive Church,
as all allow, sometimes at least gave Communion under
one kind only, it is plain that Communion under one
kind or both is a matter of discipline. When men in
danger of martyrdom were allowed to have with them
the Blessed Sacrament, it was certainly under one kind
only ; when Manicheeism condemned the use of wine,
and profaned the Mass by its omission, the Western
Church insisted on the use of bread and wine in the
Holy Sacrifice, in opposition to that heresy. Communion under both kinds continued customary in the
Eastern Communion ; Communion under one kind
became the discipline of the West, but the Church in
the West did not condemn the practice of the East,
neither did the Church in the East condemn the practice
of the West : and why ? Because the whole Church
recognised the truth that under one or other kind is
whole Christ, the Divine Person, with His entire Human
Nature, and therefore that whether under one only kind,

E

or under both, the same was received. Hence there was no difficulty in allowing the Maronites the continuance of the use of the Sacrament under both kinds; it had been their national unbroken traditional practice, and the Church of Rome showed itself tolerant of that which was time-honoured and innocent.

But the demand of Anglicans is based on heretical grounds, and the concession to the demand would be at least interpreted into an admission of the validity of those grounds. The practice of the Church of England at the time of the separation was to receive under one kind. Innovators arose who asserted that Communion under one kind was a mutilated Sacrament, that Christ was not received whole and entire under each kind, and therefore that Communion under both kinds was necessary. Hence they insisted on a change in the existing discipline, and demanded the use of the chalice equally for all. If then the Church of Rome were to concede the use of the chalice equally to all, in order to satisfy complaints founded on heretical teaching, she would practically be endorsing that heretical teaching, and so prove unfaithful to the deposit of the faith.

There was then every reason to recognise the time-honoured discipline of the Maronites, while there is an insuperable objection against conceding to Anglicans what was recognised for the Maronites. It is not necessary to remark that with regard to the use of the chalice, the Maronites during the last century adopted the discipline of the Western Church, a discipline which certainly—without blaming the contrary discipline—has the best reasons to recommend it.

It is in vain then to expect the Mother Church of the West and of the world to concede to querulous theorists points of discipline on grounds destructive of the unity of her doctrines on the plea that she allows these points to her children in the East, whose doctrine is sound.

Corporate reunion is no less practically impossible if we regard the Anglican Establishment. For those Anglicans who desire it are but a handful compared with the entire Establishment. This handful has no right to call itself the Anglican Community at the expense of the Low Church and Broad Church. All these sections use the same Prayer-book, share alike the national places of worship and the parishes, subscribe the same Articles, and protest against the same authority of the visible Head. And considered as a whole, what chance is there that these three bodies will agree on the terms of reunion, to say nothing of their agreeing even in the wish to be reunited with the Church of Rome? If then there is no reasonable hope of the Anglican body seeking reunion as a body, it is all over with corporate reunion, and the reunion of High Church Anglicans without the Low and Broad Church would only be a difference in degree, and not in kind, from the reconciliation of individuals, which is in fine the only feasible mode of reunion.

Nor if we look to the *future* can we reasonably expect such a change as would favour the fond vision of corporate reunion. Look at the so-called Bishops of the Anglican body; how many of these at the present moment have the least desire of reunion with Rome, and what hope is there of this number being

E 2

increased ? It is the lament of the unionist that it is
no longer the Sovereign but the Prime Minister that
practically appoints the Bishops. One would have
thought that it would have been sufficiently objectionable for the Sovereign to possess this extraordinary
power uncontrolled, but when the Prime Minister has
the appointment in matter of fact, and this Prime
Minister may be of any religion except the Catholic,
or of no religion at all ; when the progress of England
as a nation is certainly in the direction, not of Conservatism but of its opposite, we must conclude that
there are no cheering hopes for the future as regards
corporate reunion on the side of the Anglican Bishops ;
and yet, if reunion be corporate, none surely so much
as the Bishops ought to be regarded as the leaders and
representatives of the body. Look at the English
press ; what hope is there on this side ? Look, again,
at the seminaries of Anglicanism ; these are the Pro-
testant· Universities. More than thirty years ago there
was a move—a move in the direction of Catholicity. It
was a movement that influenced many individuals, but
it did not leaven the academic bodies, not even Oxford.
At no time was the governing body favourable to the
movement, at no time was the tutorial body in favour
of it as a body. High Church views were an objection
to tutorial appointment ; Catholicising views entailed
the refusal of Anglican ordination. The advocates of
High Church principles urged the necessity of authority,
and deference to authority was congenial to Oxford,
but not too much of it ; so long as it was confined to
a decent conservatism it was favoured, but when the
Reformation was criticised as an offence against autho-

rity, when the necessity of acknowledging an infallible authority was maintained, then its defenders found that they were really a "foreign body" in the University, out of their place and giving uneasiness. Then it was that those who had caught a glimpse of the meaning of Catholic unity submitted to the voice of the Chief Pastor, and were reconciled to the Catholic Church. Others less logical, or for other reasons, remained where they were and carried on a losing game. They in time left the University for livings in the country and for domestic life ; their pupils took their degrees and received Anglican ordination, and they carried into the parishes where they were fixed love of ceremonial, works of benevolence, and a travesty of Catholicity, and it is they who represent the Catholicising element in Anglicanism now. But where are there Catholicising successors to take their place ? The Universities are not now possessed of Catholicising teachers ; "Puseyism," as men call it, is in Oxford dying out or dead, and the parish Rectors, Vicars, and Curates of the next generation will be no longer advocates of corporate reunion.

Neither the present or the future, then, gives any grounds for the opinion that corporate reunion is possible. The Church of Christ would be faithless to her trust if she made concessions which are demanded by innovators still calling themselves her reformers, and which are demanded on the presumption of her having mutilated the Sacraments. Anglicans as a body neither desire reunion nor is it likely that as a body they ever will ; Low Church and Broad Church will never join the High Church in its fond scheme. And things will

not change for the better. Look to the Bishops, look
to the press, look to the Universities, and there is
nothing before Anglicans but a dreary waste and
hopeless degeneracy.

Finally, Anglican Orders can never be admitted as
certainly valid, and therefore can never be admitted at
all. Were they merely doubtful, the Catholic Church
could not associate Protestant Clergymen with her
Priests, and the idea of amalgamating Anglican Bishops
with the hierarchy of England is not only out of the
question but is grotesque. Were the ordination of
Anglican Ministers merely doubtful, the act of consecration in the Communion service would be doubtful
too, and the Church of Christ could not sanction or
tolerate the probably material idolatry which would be
the consequence.

Alas! for the time wasted in elaborating theories to
make the worse appear the better reason, to clothe
schism in the garb of integrity, and persuade men
against the evidence of their senses either that the
Anglican body forms one Church with the Catholic,
or that, if it does not, it is lawfully though lamentably
separated from it, and that the time of corporate
reunion ought to be waited for, while multitudes of
individuals are tampering with their consciences, or at
least—if they are in good faith—are being deprived by
their false guides of the graces which flow from the
Blood of Jesus Christ, through the Sacraments of His
Church.

In the midst of all, the Spouse of Christ can only
look on sorrowfully while she remonstrates with the
deceived, and tells them that when they have gone

through every change of argument that human inge-- nuity can devise, they will find her at the end always the same, praying for their recovery, and longing to receive them back into her bosom.

In these lectures the attempt has been made to state without prejudice the case between Anglicanism and Catholicity. Much time and labour are spent by earnest souls on disputation and historical research, but they must return at last, like little children, to the Apostles' Creed—"I believe the Holy Catholic Church;" and they will find the unity implied in that Article nowhere but in that Church which is loyal to Pius IX., the successor of St. Peter and the Vicar of Christ.

www.ingramcontent.com/pod-product-compliance
Lightning Source LLC
Chambersburg PA
CBHW021542270326
41930CB00008B/1337